A Book of Kisses

Cameron Roy

Dear Sid

May you come
to realize
the love that you are.

Loving
Cam

Copyright

Cover art © Deborah Koff-Chapin 2016 touchdrawing.com

Cover designed by Cameron Roy, Shara Morales, and Danielle Storzuk.

Back cover photography by Angela Stearns.

Cameron Roy

First Printing: December 2018
Silver Droplets Publishing Ltd.

Dedication

To the beautiful spirit that is Shara Morales.

Contents

Words of Appreciation

"You are the burning fire
that weaves poetry into life."
~ Shara Morales ~

"Written from the heart and what you see through
your eyes. It is a good way of looking at love."
~ Anonymous ~

"Your poetry is beautiful! Your words elicit feeling
and sensation in a soft and enticing way."
~ Deonesea La Fey ~

"Each poem has a special meaning and gets your
imagination going. When reading them myself they gave
me a warm feeling and yet my mind was thinking this is
how I sometimes feel."
~ Kim Johnson ~

"Beautiful Cameron Roy. Your poetry is that... poetry. Pure and touching. A must read journey of love and kisses."

~ Laura Heselton ~

"Thank you very much for your story, I send you with deep tenderness and passion kisses."

~ Eden ~

Foreword

A book of Kisses is the journey of the skin awakening to a higher consciousness. Each poem is crafted with such a presence that has the power to immerse the reader in the lushness of being alive. Aware of the smallest of sensations: the expectancy of a contact, the coming closer together and the lingering imprints it has left - every step delicately observed and masterfully enlarged for us to rest in it, to take delight in the fullness of a single instant.

Back in October 2011, when Cameron Roy was still living in the cool sobriety of Zurich, we sat together at a cozy café to brainstorm – or rather heartstorm – the contents of his next speech at Toastmasters. I admit it: when I casually mentioned, "Why don't you talk about kisses?" – a topic that I secretly wanted to develop myself. I could have never imagined the depth and height he would get to reach in his undertaking. I should have seen it coming though, given that since the very first moment I met Cameron I have been blessed to witness his unending creative juices flowing towards beauty, sensitivity and joy. He started his Toastmaster speech with a question...

"Why We Kiss"

He found out that a kiss triggers a cascade of neural messages and chemicals that transmit tactile sensations, sexual excitement, feelings of closeness, motivation and even euphoria. That human lips enjoy the slimmest layer of skin on the human body, and that the lips are among the most densely populated with sensory neurons of any region of the body. So when we kiss, these neurons, rocket messages to the brain setting off delightful sensations, intense emotions and physical reactions.

"One dance,
one look,
one kiss,
that's all we get...
one shot,
to make the difference
between love
and 'Oh?
That's just someone I knew before,' "

he said playfully during his presentation.

A kiss is that powerful.

So much information is exchanged with a kiss, that one kiss can change everything; it's the ultimate litmus test in a relationship. When we kiss, it is something that we tend to do without much thought, we just do it.

We are drawn by desire, pleasure – our impulse. Yet, in Cameron's case it is definitely not an unconscious event, quite the opposite, it is a fully aware one, brave and magnificent in its utter simplicity; each short poem with a slightly different view point, each including a small evolution of an adult human being with a vivid inner life.

It all began with a kiss.
It really began before that
to come to a point
to have that first kiss
where I kissed your fingers
delicately, softly and
with undeniable power.

Cameron Roy is a man in perpetual artistic creation; one could say that "life" is his canvas. Above all, for me, he embodies an underlying love and devotion.

"Since feeling is first" From a poem by E. E. Cummings, *"kisses are a better fate than wisdom."* In Cameron Roy's work we find both, fate and wisdom, because he soaks each word with awareness and goes beyond the kissing lips to hint at that royal presence, the one "actually experiencing."

Caress of the lips
send shivers
cells tingling.

A book of Kisses is the expression of a man that has devoted his life to the path of living eyes wide open. In this path, Cameron Roy gives the body a soulful place. So much that the caress, the actual kiss, inevitably point towards the greatest mystery, that which some would call Life, Creator, The Infinite, God, or as the mystic poet Rumi would utter softly: The Beloved.

And so we close with a kiss,

Shara Morales
Zurich, 17.08.2018

Preface

YES, THIS IS A BOOK OF POETRY, OF KISSES, really it is more, much more... it is a journey, a journey of love, sex, romance and spirit that guides us all.

The Journey

There is no greater journey
than the journey of love
it is full of pitfalls, dangers and rewards
there is no winning or losing
there is no cup, no grail
there is only the journey
only the love
and the choices
that we make along the way.

From the felt experience of the journey of love, our love unfolded, evolved. Burning Heart met Living Canvas in the South of France at a retreat centre for an intensive week-long process, we were both in the throes of heartbreak.

Living Canvas, "you opened a mysterious door in front of my eyes."

Burning Heart, "oh? do say more."

Living Canvas, "and like a magician you started to bring light to your soul-creations... you can see in me far beyond what I can see. What you touch in you, you touch in me, and this is truly mysterious. You know how to play the cords of a puppet that enter a fantastic life when it is in your hands, putting life in your touch courageously. I will never forget how you took my hand and kissed my fingers, gently but also with a sharp edge kindly, but with un-denying power."

Who is Burning Heart and Living Canvas you may ask?

Burning Heart is me, and as young man I wrote poetry to girls that I had a crush on, to my first love, and my hairdresser. Later finding a soul mate in my ex-wife. Living Canvas is my present beloved, my muse, inspiration and connection to an essence of soul expression that is reflected back to me and through another human mirror.

One day after doing a process together Living Canvas asked...

"do you think we'll fall in love?"

My mind was quiet for a moment then spontaneously and innocently I said "yes, I'm sure we will", my thought was "do you mean you and I?" What a beautiful initial spark of possibility and opening of light in the pain of heartbreak. One month later we met for lunch, talking, feeling a bit awkward at first then a shift, into a different place, timeless space in our own bubble.

Six months later, Living Canvas said to me "I feel your presence, your strength and sense of self emerging stronger. Like steel being tempered, into the fire and into the cold. You have green eyes, manifesting as lake of deep stillness."

A Book of Kisses is a journey, from the throes of heartbreak to the depth and truth of love. Let us be swept away, my beloved, in the passionate loving that renders duality into one, and tips the mind into ecstasy.

Burning Heart with Living Canvas and beyond, come with me on this journey. Like most great love stories, it began with a kiss. It all began with a kiss, when I kissed your fingers...

Burning Heart, "I have finally met someone who has the depth, passion, feeling... to go with me into those places."

Living Canvas, "I have to admit that I felt I was stronger, but you seduce me and my mind just stops, it is as if you had keys."

Burning Heart, "I am also surprised at the depth of experience, the depth of passion that I feel with you, the places we can go."

Living Canvas, "I am surprised too."

I give you a kiss
I am met there by you
in your kiss
in that moment
I met you
time stood still
our hearts in joyful union
after our kiss
back to myself
connected to you.

To my readers from Burning Heart. I am a mystic, like Rumi, and as a mystic I write poetry that is beyond the truth of the intellect, I write from the felt sense of experience on love, romance, sex and spirituality.

Welcome to the heart of my soul.

How to Read This Book

Being a book of poetry is an invitation to the senses,
to dive into your inner world, it's about feeling first,
heartfelt and soulful.

Sit quietly with a cup of tea, a blanket in the soft
stillness of night, pause, take a breath and allow your
heart to select a page, a poem.

Share it with your lover, your friend, or just yourself.
Take turns to select a poem and read to each other,
delighting in the feeling, sensation evoked from within.

There is no right way to read this book, as there is no
wrong way, these are merely suggestions, possible
paths, the choice is yours. Choose your way.

The Journey

There is no greater journey
than the journey of love
it is full of pitfalls and rewards
there is no winning or losing
there is no cup, no grail
there is only the journey
only the love
and the choices
that we make along the way.

It All Began

It all began with a kiss.
It really began before that
to come to a point
to have that first kiss
where I kissed your fingers
delicately, softly and
with undeniable power.

Fleeting Thought

Faster than a fleeting thought
I'll be out of this world.

May You

May you come
to realize
the love that you are.

Truth

There is the truth
then there is the path
of how we get there.

Unknown

How does the unknown
become known?
By going there.

Come Dance with Me

Come dance with me
in the dance of life
a life together.
A journey of discovery,
of ourselves and each other
in the bed, under the sheets
Dance of pleasure,
passion and ecstasy
tango,
leading, following
yielding
into the light.

Intimate Journey

Let us go on an intimate journey of two
a journey of discovery of ourselves
and each other
an intimate journey of love
me and you
you and me
let us dance between the sheets
in our passion
the tango of life
dancing in the streets
let us sing our song
creating our music together.

Love is Strange

Love is strange
no, love is mysterious and beautiful
this force that brings people together
this force that binds and runs the universe
all of creation
love is all that there is.

I Give You a Kiss

I give you a kiss
a gentle caress on the lips
reaching into your heart
into your soul
and down, down,
down to your toes
I give you a kiss.

I Want You

I want you
today
tomorrow
next week
next month
next year and beyond
to bring a smile to your heart
to touch you
deeply.

First Kiss

As a first kiss should be
fresh, exciting
leaving you thrilled
wanting more.

Gift

I give you the gift of myself
may I have the honour
the pleasure
to bring joy
and love to your heart
every day, in every way.

Butterfly Kiss

A soft and delicate kiss
as if a butterfly is landing on your skin
delicate and soft
to awaken your senses
I am here with you
my lips
in communion
with your skin.

Robust Kiss

A delicate robust kiss
softly, slowly,
lingering on your lips
the full sensuality
resonating
permeating your being.

I Met You

I give you a kiss
I am met there by you
in your kiss
in that moment
I met you
time stood still
our hearts in joyful union
after our kiss
back to myself
connected to you.

Strength Rising

The Phoenix was down, not out
thru the tears
the flames of surrender
vulnerable, revealed,
healing, emerging,
rising again.
The strength, always known
now rising from within,
present, foreground
the phoenix resurrected
strength emanating from within.

Frame

My frame
my game!

Los Colores

Vibrant colours
rising, swirling, intense.
Your essence shining
vulnerable
rich with potential
flowing in the dance of contact
meeting and being met in your space
seen, revealed – "los colores"
shining thru
holding the tension
following impulse
a leap with excitement
withdrawing back to yourself
small, curled up.
Impulse
holding space,
contained, sustained.

Fresh out of the Shower

You emerge out of the shower
wrapped in a towel
fresh and clean,
so inviting.
I come behind you
to kiss the back of your neck.
Saying I love you
you are so beautiful
do we have time to make love?
I take you now
a strong and passionate kiss
pulling you close
pressing our bodies together.

Kiss with an Edge

A kiss with an edge
gently with my teeth
with an edge
power smoldering
just beneath the surface
controlled and wild
the tiger and the tigress.

Good Night Kiss

A good night kiss
sensation lingering
on your lips
radiating tension
in your body
to take with you
into your dreams.

Good Morning Kiss

A good morning kiss
that says hello,
to begin the day
awakening from sleep
slumber
dream land
hello, I want you
I'm here with you
desire
a fresh kiss
clean and pure
with the rhythm awakening
feeling warmth and closeness of our bodies.

Soul Kiss

Lying next to each other
gazing deep
into each other's eyes
into your soul.

Strength and Surrender

The soft delicate kisses and caresses
that awaken all of your senses
electric.
Surrender to the wildly sensuous experience
a celebration
playing the body from the heart
and into the soul.
Like the finest musician and his instrument
you and I the two become one
imminent destiny
coaxing and caressing
producing and creating
in the eternal flow
the sweetest music a body has ever felt
quivering
quivering waves of sensation
diving into the divine
riding the wave
of ecstatic joy.

Caress

I give you a kiss
my hand
on your tummy
feel the warmth
my strength
the presence of my touch
a caress – my energy
my heat gently permeating
penetrating your skin
your muscles, your cells
your body loving it, melting
an infinite caress
that lingers
your body remembers
as my caress glides over your skin
a shiver.

Present with You

I give you a kiss
present with you
present in my kiss and caress
present with you in an infinite caress
pulling you close to kiss
a gentle caress on the lips
a gentle bite, a kiss with an edge
our bodies singing
so alive in the moment
there is only you and I
our heart and soul
soaring in the eternal bliss
creating our celestial music.

Hold You

When can I hold you again
kiss you
see the radiant beauty of your smile
gaze softly in your eyes
into your soul.

Birthday Kiss

I give you a kiss
a birthday kiss
that says I celebrate you
the beauty
the creation that is you.

Knowledge and Mystery

My mysterious beauty
as I discover you
know you
I realize that there is always more to know
that the journey of knowing you
discovering you is mysterious and beautiful.
I love the journey as I love you.
I love the journey of discovering you
knowing you
loving you.

Infinite Kiss

An infinite kiss
time stands still
the world slips away
melting, dissolving
hearts joining
in our bubble.

Glittering Snow Dust

Out the window
the glittering snow dust
beckons me softly
icicles sparkling
tiny stars of ice just born
sparkling and glittering
brought alive by the sun
crisp, cold, frozen
in the solitude of a cutting wind
I remain within
how can you be so inviting
when it is freezing?
Fascinatingly beautiful
untouchable
amidst the bright blue sky
a crystal halo of light
shimmering softly
unreachable.

Playfully Sweet

I give you a kiss
strong and tender
infinite and deep
playfully sweet.

A Snow Day

In the snow
you make your way
your smile makes my day!

Subtle Vibration

I give you a kiss
softly on your forehead
as you lie with your head in my lap
caressing your hair
decadent indulgence
subtle vibration
emanating from deep within
listening to the music heard so deeply
surrender to the moment
to the deep caress
that lingers, and goes on,
and on, and on.

Sweet and Intense

I give you a kiss
sweet and intense
delicately strong
luscious and lingering.

Good Night

Lying in bed
I snuggle up behind you, you melt into me
soft and warm skin on skin
your breath as it moves you
my breath, deep, filling my chest
our breath, breathing us
slow, unhurried kisses on the back of your neck
feel my breath purring
my hand wrapped around
resting on your tummy
emanating warmth into your core
the soft warmth, tingling
listening, present with you
softening, slowing down, softly sinking
breath and body becoming easeful
whispering sweetly in your ear
"I love you, Je Taime, Agapo"
the soft waves coming, rolling gently
carrying us off into sleep.

Caress of the Lips

Caress of the lips
sends shivers
cells pulsating.

Sparkling Smile

Sparkling smile
eyes bright
radiant expression.

Keen Mind

Keen mind
absorbing it all
thirst to know more
weaver of knowledge
storyteller.

Delicate Strength

Delicate strength
soft rumbling
awakens.

Red

Red
juicy succulent red
strawberry
watermelon
ripe.

Sweet

Love
sweet love
when it truly happens
is precious.

Cresting the Wave

Sharp breath
a gasp
cresting the wave.

Vibrating

How happy we are
vibrating
sparkling
creating.

Magic

We create magic.
How else can you describe
the love that we share.
When it comes together
your love and my love
mixed together
we create something
magic.
We fly without a broomstick
we fly and soar thru the heavens
thru the emotions
with wings, the journey of our soul
into our hearts
we fly.

I Hold You

I hold you close
I hold you strong
in a place
where you belong.

Your Flower

Your flower
opening
blooming
to reveal its sweet nectar
inviting me in.

Waking

Upon waking
I felt you.

Spring Green

Spring green
tender shoot
emerging.

Breaking Free

For the emerging YOU
I see you
breaking free
young green shoot
delicate and strong
standing on your own
struggling to break free.
For the emerging you
spiraling
I see you
young green shoot
delicate and strong
standing on your own
transformed.

Emerging

Emerging
the woman
the goddess
butterfly
writer
creator.

Seven Ways

Seven ways to love you
"only seven?" you ask.
No, only one
with my heart.

I Love You

I love you
not because I want to
simply because
I do.

Where are you?

When you were away
the days went on
"where are you?"
I call out.
Opening my wallet
I saw your picture.

Why do I Love You

I love you
sometimes I ask myself why?
I come up with many reasons
yet that isn't it.
What is the real reason
what is the essence of my love for you?
As I reflected on my question
the answer came to me
my emotion, my feeling
I do, I just do
my heart opens
my love flows to you.

Hearts Expanding

A deep lingering kiss
little love bites on your neck
held in an infinite caress
a soft gaze, self revealed
energies combining
a juicy creation
blissful dance, awakening
pulsating
vibrating
fire building
the deep heat
our hearts expanding into union.

Exotic

Our love mixed together
creativity stirred
exotic
manifestation.

Reflecting

I was reflecting on our love this morning
"Do I love you more now than when we met?"
At first I said yes, then no, then...
I went back in time
our love began from the moment we met
a spark, delight, magic bubble
into strong currents of passion
deep emotion, connected
thru romance, idolization and some stormy waters
building our own ground, interdependent
and continues to deepen and flourish.
My thoughts turn to the ocean, vast and deep
so many nooks and crannies to explore
abundant, interesting
the more I explore, the more I know you
the deeper I go into you
into our love, an ever evolving spiral.

Breath of Life

I kiss you so hard
I take your breath away
and breathe
the breath of life
back into you
again.

Friends, Lovers, Soul Mates

We are friends
lovers, soul mates
and more, much more...
Rare and exquisite
to be soul mates
together in this world
together again
together.
Our relationship, our love
is a great love
and continues to grow
deeper, richer, stronger
exquisite.

Driving Home

Driving home
I look up to see the moon
full and plump in a harvest glow
you're in my thoughts
so close, I can touch you
Living Canvas writing in my Burning Heart
my love flowing on a moon beam to you
I know what I want
your lips on mine!

Merging

Merging, not lost in the other
merging into the divine
becoming more than we are.

Reverberating in Sacred Space

I give you a kiss
a gentle caress of the lips
reaching into your heart
reverberating in sacred space
cells tingling
all the way down
to your toes
I give you a kiss
your flower opening
to reveal it's sweet nectar
exquisite beauty
unfolding, emerging
met by your kiss
sweet softness
sensual space
creating together
passionately.

Inner Space

Inner space
softly waiting
silently emerging
becoming defined, refined
in exquisite beauty
unfolding strength
stepping thru the doorway
a gate that has been waiting
flickering, a glimpse
now becoming known
running freely
exhilarating
a taste of wildness
thundering earth
shimmering sky
softness and space
creative expression
bubbling forth.

Lips United

Our first kiss
lips united
a heady rush.

Rivulets of Pleasure

Gliding caress
rivulets of pleasure
dancing beneath your skin.

Waves

Waves
building
cresting
crashing
sensations
deep
within.

Vibrant Vitality

Vibrant vitality
love burning bright.

My Special One

A soft kiss on the cheek
gathering attention.
A tender kiss on your forehead
my special one.
Juicy lips
inviting
igniting passion
drawing me in.

Ethereal

Ghost of spirit
ethereal
the body subtle
spirit condensed.

I Feel without Words

I feel without words
my pen quietly waits
what is this lull?
For one who is filled with passion
in my centre I am still and quiet
joy bubbling forth
how do I put down in words
how wonderful life is now that
you are in the world.

Melting

Liquid manna
exploding inside
bathed in golden light
melting from within
boundaries dissolved
surrender to our union
bliss comes over us.

Entwined

Deeply entwined in a kiss
your heart in mine
touching the divine.

Cake

Super yummy cake
made by you, just for two
a precious moment shared
on a bench by a busy street
full with timeless space
you are here in my arms again
all is right in the world
a magical moment in time
an aha moment, our brightness
delightful eternal spark
synergistic alchemy
alive, thriving in this mystical magic union
solar flares from deep within our core
aha, it is you and I
what we create together.
Effortlessly, moulding, melting
spiraling, circling in drawn by our lips
magnetic pull into our kiss.

Love Lives On

I'd die for you
surrender
I live in you
and you in me
for there is no death in love
our love lives on.

In Bloom

The flower of our hearts
in bloom
my love
flourishes in you.

Turn

If no one turns on the light
are we not all in the dark?

I Give You a Kiss

I give you a kiss

loooooooooooooooooong

l
u
s
c
i
o
u
s

l i n g e r i n g

Transition

Thru the gate
in the field of creation
playfully bringing into existence
transitioning
another gate to be opened.

Threshold

I pick you up
carry you across the threshold
thru the door
into our life together.

Becoming

I want you
today, tomorrow and beyond
day to day
the perfections and imperfections
becoming.
To know you deeply, intimately
love you truly.
I open the gate
the gate to my heart
I open myself to you
come in, come in
come in to our flow
to our life together.

We Touch

Forehead to forehead, we touch
it is you, whom I love so much
listening intently
heart flutter
bubbly delight
circling round and round
streaming light.

Forever

I share with you
my heart, my love
forever in a day.

How do you Feel

How do you feel
when a soul lights up
another sparks.

Awake in the Night

Awake
in the night with you
bright light
rich night.

Fiercely Male

Fiercely male
I blaze a trail!

Light

I am light
I am love
I evolve.

Wonderful You

I thought of you
I imagined you
I saw you, I see you
alive, beautiful, free
the wonderful you that you are.

Tibits

An evening at Tibits
full
a wonderful evening with you
full in our hearts
dancing in places to go
creating as we go
creating to and fro
full and bright like the moon
shimmering clouds
in a soft glow.

Deep Peace

Feel the deep peace
within you
touching grace.

Mille Bisous Pour Toi

1001 bisous pour toi
partout
dans ton corps.

The Deep Ache

The deep ache
longing
you need me
inside.

The Hubris of Man

Therein lies the hubris of man
thinking he is great alone.

Beautiful Distraction

Distracted
so in love
my thoughts
return to you
again and again.

Holding Your Heart

Holding your heart
in my hands
embracing
your heart of hearts.

Goddess in a Toga

Goddess in a toga
by the seaside
a fiery hot male
may I kiss you?
an explosion of light.

Burning Heart

Burning Heart
a mystic
touching people's hearts
it's who you are that counts
the love that you live
the love you leave behind.

Green Mountain

My Yang
your Yin.
Green mountain
let the kissing begin.

Darkness to Light

The darkness envelopes me
even in this darkness there is light.
Deep indigo of the third eye
lighting my way.
I can see far enough to take a step
a candle appears
climb, climb out, up the stairs
I step into my heart
sparkling light.
Still, there is a darkness behind me
I turn to face the darkness
What's here? What do I see?
An old scene.
A new scene becomes illuminated
filled with angel's grace.

Dancing Flame

A candle lit, two flames, our light, dancing
in sync, in unison, one heart to another
"duende", sparking one another
burning bright, separate and together
lead and follow, the dance of souls
united
is the candle separate from the flame
am I separate from my love
I am in my love and she is in me
we continue into infinity
for am I me and you are you
burning bright into the night
dawn's early light
safely held
opening doors within
this is our light
dancing flame of love.

Quiet Mind

Hard to be Zen
blank state
quiet mind.

Blank State

Hard to be Zen
blank state
quiet mind
space for nothing
to become something.

Festival of Colours

A festival of colours
celebrating
you and I
the colours of our love.

Soft Glow

I pick you up
squeezing tight
in the soft glow
of the moonlight.

Moon Beam

Under the stars
warm summer night
sparkling
waves lapping on the shore
tickling our feet
coming to you on a moon beam
I go to the window
the moon in it's pale glow
my heart talking to yours.

Dreaming

Missing you
burning for you
listening to your dreams
the night dreams
unconscious being made conscious
what you are living and learning.
The dreams of your heart, your soul
what you desire
that which you aspire to.

Comfort Zone

Move out of your comfort zone
to where life happens.

Our Love

Our love
written in the sky
you and I.

Receive

Receive a kiss
soft, slow
full of glow.

River of My Heart

River of my heart
gently flows
from me to you
we light up
with each other
sparkling, dancing, light
driving, talking
before my words reach you
you hear my soul speak
look into your eyes
gaze into your soul
touched
a joyful tear.

To my Love

I give you the gift of myself
I give you my love
today I ask you
may I?
May I have the honour and the pleasure?
To bring knowledge and mystery to your curious mind
to bring passionate fire to your emotions
to bring rapturous pleasure to your body
to bring love to your soul
to bring a smile to your heart
to bring joy, love, light and laughter to your being.
Today, tomorrow,
next week, next month,
next year and beyond.
Will you join me on the infinite journey of love?
On the journey of our love
will you?

Te Amo

When I see you, think of you
I want to know you thru and thru.
The lotus flower symbol of opening
of divinity that which I see blossoming
in you and me.
Though we may be far apart in the coming months
in my heart you are near, you are here
deeply connected in love and life
beauty and passion
knowledge and mystery
transformation
independence and union
and on, and on, and on...
I love you
"Te amo".

Sparkling

Sparkling, awakening
I touch you, I feel you
your kiss lingering
on my lips
I feel
the smile
in your heart.

Linked

Linked thru time
your heart in mine.

Soulmates

How divine
the stories we have weaved
together thru time
the irresistible tug
of your soul to mine.

Window

Last night
I dreamt of you
a window
to your soul.

Dance

A quiet dance in the light
softly we go
into the night.

Look

Look into my eyes
the eyes of an artist
expressing my soul
to you.

Tired of a Long Day

Tired of a long day
it's on your face
coming home
unwind
be present with me
eyes softening
dropping into grace
back into you.

Devotion

Devotion
beyond commitment
obligation no more.

Thrive

Thrive
beyond I would die for you
I thrive with you.

Lotus Flower Blooming

Lotus flower blooming
petals unfurled
pristine, fresh
unfolding
in a still pool.

Still Water

Each drop
connecting
becoming whole.

Intoxicating Mixture

A potion an elixir, intoxicating mixture
a heart that loves without fixture.
How long? How long till I see you again?
Born from an open heart
deep bond that goes beyond
where your innermost feelings
can be known, is shown
flourishing in an eternal
fountain of light
you called, I came
to you, my flame
your heart called mine
the struggle to meet you
in the constraints of space and time
our hearts won
the call of the heart stronger
they long, they pull us
guide us to be one.

You Thrive

You thrive
together, we come alive
a spiraling mix
of dancing flame.

Living Canvas

Living Canvas
what does she express?
A right to exist.

Creative Something

A creative something
inspired
wired!

Infused

On your way out
we meet
a bright smile
infused
infused with the spirit
of you.

Hot Yoga

Pushing us
to our edge
falling
into grace.

Improv

Life is the ultimate creation
improv of life.

Normal

What is normal?
No one is
we are who we are.

Surfacing

Surface of awareness
moves and flows
deep emotion
sentient being
in the know.

Creation

To creation
ever new
discovering
that which is inside of you
the impulse that lives.

Change it Up

Change it up
engage awareness
become alive.

Kissing your Breast

I kiss your breast
close to your heart
I kiss your lips
we meet again.

Love's Potion

Devotion
love's potion
intoxicating elixir.

Experience

Experience
does something
to your soul.

Heart of Hearts

Into your heart of hearts
go there
meet me
be still.

Your Heart

Your heart
flowing
knowing
cup of love
growing.

Cup of Love

Cup of love
fiery soul
blazing
trekking
from my heart
to yours
whole.

Your Centre

Your centre
heart of hearts
all of you.

To the Edge

To the edge
not on a ledge
falling, falling
leaping
diving
into grace.

Waiting

Wanting, waiting
anticipating
when will he begin?

Half Moon

Half moon
shining bright
hidden behind.

Shallow Breath

Shallow breath
in sync
the movement of your body
ignites sparks in mine.

Super Nova

Super nova
bright, beautiful
filled with light!

Celebrate

I celebrate you
the day you were born
this day, today
your parents
the heavens
your impulse to be!

Super Moon

Tonight is a super Moon
an eclipse
and a blood Moon
it comes rarely.

Holding Space

I hold space
for you to be.

My Fire

My fire
contains
your flame.

Kizomba

Present
in timeless space
floating
on my wings.

To the Light

A certain fascination with the darkness
holds me from getting thru to the light
I am on my way
sweet surrender
to the light
travelling
the dark corners of ourselves.

Soul Travelers

Soul travelers
on waves of the heart
riding the ebb and flow.

Nature's Embrace

In nature's embrace
a mountain stream
deep in the forest
solitude
renewed.

Ecstasy

Ecstasy of surrender
diffuse awareness dissolved.

Far Away

Although you are far away
you are here, near
here, in my soul.

Thread of Love

Another year
has come and gone
our love remains strong
thread of love unites
in resonance
with the flow of life.

Magnetic Pull

Your heart to mine
magnetic
a moth to a flame
how long?
How long till I see you again?

Acknowledgements

I would like to thank Shara for the idea to write about kisses. Creative genius, co-creator extraordinaire, ideas flow effortlessly with you. For your support, inspiration, encouragement, challenging me, and most of all for your love.

I am grateful for Laura working with me on how to manifest, visioning, connecting the dots and providing clarity in starting this quest, this journey.

Setting course, how the path unfolds connecting me with Selina and her Curious Courses and introducing me to Edson Williams and his Lead by Example program. To Edson for helping me get clear on my life purpose, leading by example, flipping the script and challenging me in coaching sessions.

I would like to thank Gilly for her friendship, sharing deeply, traveling the turbulent waters of emotion and being a steady guide along the way. Our Soul Card sessions at the Omega Institute in Rhineback and beyond, the Soul Card images tapping into the deeper realms.

I appreciate Deborah Koff-Chapin and the Center for Touch Drawing for the exquisite cover art.

To Siegmar and Cornelia for their support, guidance, teaching and unconditional love when I was broken.

I am grateful to Christine, the love of my life, soul mate, who believed in me.

Thank you to the Toastmasters Club of Zurich for the forum, coaching and support to develop my public speaking, the place where my speech "Why we Kiss" came to life. Along with William and John for their coaching, support, feedback and most of all their friendship.

A heart felt thank you Danielle, fellow writer, poet and soul traveler for her friendship, honest feedback and editing.

For my fellow brothers in Bear Squad for holding space, support and accountability. Ho!

A big thank you to Traci, for the Ringmaster program, bringing the vision back into focus, getting clear on the why, setting goals and the structure to make steady progress.

I am grateful for Phil T. Mistlberger diving into the shadow realms, clearing shame, helping me to find my edge and fire.

All of the goddesses who I connect with on a heart level, these poems are about you, for you, to celebrate the light within, the depths of your heart connecting with you in your heart of hearts.

Thank you Yogi Jodie, creating a family, a loving space and all of your Jodie'isms that we love so much. I am grateful for my yoga family, the morning Yoga crew where ideas percolate.

Last but not last Thank you Michele, small town Saskatchewan meets big city New Yorker, that's all I'm gonna say about that.

Made in the USA
Middletown, DE
25 March 2019